Earth's Landforms and Bodies of Water

Natalie Hyde

Crabtree Publishing Company
www.crabtreebooks.com

Author
Natalie Hyde

Publishing plan research and development
Reagan Miller

Editor
Crystal Sikkens

Proofreader and indexer
Wendy Scavuzzo

Design
Samara Parent

Photo research
Tammy McGarr

Prepress technician
Tammy McGarr

Print and production coordinator
Margaret Amy Salter

Photographs
Shutterstock: p14 © Gilles Paire
Thinkstock: p19

All other images from Shutterstock

Library and Archives Canada Cataloguing in Publication

Hyde, Natalie, 1963-, author
    Earth's landforms and bodies of water / Natalie Hyde.

(Earth's processes close-up)
Includes index.
Issued in print and electronic formats.
ISBN 978-0-7787-1723-2 (bound).--ISBN 978-0-7787-1745-4 (paperback).--
ISBN 978-1-4271-1608-6 (pdf).--ISBN 978-1-4271-1604-8 (html)

    1. Landforms--Juvenile literature. 2. Bodies of water--Juvenile literature.
3. Earth (Planet)--Surface--Juvenile literature. 4. Physical geography--Juvenile
literature. I. Title.

GB58.H94 2015   j551   C2015-903922-3
                                      C2015-903923-1

Library of Congress Cataloging-in-Publication Data

Hyde, Natalie, 1963-
    Earth's landforms and bodies of water / Natalie Hyde.
        pages cm. -- (Earth's processes close-up)
    Includes index.
    ISBN 978-0-7787-1723-2 (reinforced library binding) --
ISBN 978-0-7787-1745-4 (pbk.) --
ISBN 978-1-4271-1608-6 (electronic pdf) --
ISBN 978-1-4271-1604-8 (electronic html)
    1. Landforms--Juvenile literature. 2. Bodies of water--Juvenile literature. 3.
Earth (Planet)--Surface--Juvenile literature. I. Title.
    GB404.H94 2016
    551.41--dc23
                        2015024021

Crabtree Publishing Company

Printed in Canada/092020/BF20200814

www.crabtreebooks.com   1-800-387-7650

Copyright © **2016 CRABTREE PUBLISHING COMPANY**. All rights reserved. No part of this publication may be reproduced, stored in a retrieval system or be transmitted in any form or by any means, electronic, mechanical, photocopying, recording, or otherwise, without the prior written permission of Crabtree Publishing Company. In Canada: We acknowledge the financial support of the Government of Canada through the Canada Book Fund for our publishing activities.

Published in Canada
Crabtree Publishing
616 Welland Ave.
St. Catharines, Ontario
L2M 5V6

Published in the United States
Crabtree Publishing
PMB 59051
350 Fifth Avenue, 59th Floor
New York, New York 10118

Published in the United Kingdom
Crabtree Publishing
Maritime House
Basin Road North, Hove
BN41 1WR

Published in Australia
Crabtree Publishing
3 Charles Street
Coburg North
VIC 3058

Contents

Land and water   4

Rocky planet   6

Raised landforms   8

Low landforms   10

Land near water   12

Where is water found on Earth?   14

Frozen solid   16

Models of Earth   18

Making models   20

Studying Earth   22

Learning more   23

Words to know and Index   24

Land and water

Our planet Earth is home to plants, animals, and humans. They live on land and in the water. Earth's surface is not the same everywhere. It has mountains, hills, valleys, plains, and plateaus. These shapes on Earth's surface are called landforms. Earth also has streams, lakes, ponds, and oceans. These are called bodies of water.

Mountains are the highest landforms on Earth's surface.

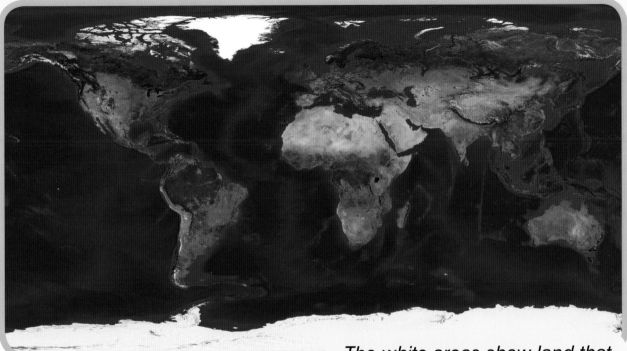

The white areas show land that is frozen for most of the year.

Mapping Earth

We can study landforms and bodies of water on a map. A map is a model of Earth. A model is a **representation** of a real object. Look at the map on this page. The blue areas show where water is found on Earth. What do you think the others colors show?

Rocky planet

Earth's land is made up of rocks. That is why it is called a rocky planet. The biggest pieces of rock form mountains. Boulders are huge rocks that break off mountains. Sometimes the rock has been crushed into smaller pieces. Gravel is made up of small stones and pebbles. Gravel is used on roads and to make **concrete**. Tiny pieces of rocks and minerals make sand. Beaches are made of sand.

Concrete is strong enough to hold up cars, trains, and buildings.

Where things grow

Soil is the loose top layer of Earth's surface. It is made up of rocks, minerals, and bits of dead plants and animals.

Can a mountain become sand over time? Why or why not?

Plants grow in soil.

Raised landforms

There are many different kinds of landforms on Earth. Some landforms are raised. This means they are higher than the area of land around them. Mountains are the highest raised landforms on Earth. They have **steep**, sloping sides. A group of mountains in the same area is called a mountain range.

peak

The sides of a mountain meet at a point at the top called the peak.

Plateaus can be thousands of feet high.

What do you think?

How is a plateau different from a mountain?
How is a plateau different from a hill?

High ground

A hill is smaller than a mountain. Hills have rounded tops. A plateau is also a raised landform. It rises high above the land around it. A plateau has a flat surface on the top. It is surrounded by steep sides called cliffs.

9

Low landforms

The Grand Canyon in Arizona is one of the largest canyons in the world.

Some landforms are lower than the land around them. Valleys are a kind of low landform. They are usually found between raised landforms. Water runs down the sides of mountains and hills. It wears away rock and soil at the bottom. This creates a valley. A canyon is deeper than a valley. It is narrow and has very steep sides. It is cut out by a fast-moving river.

Flat landforms

Some landforms are neither high nor low. A plain is a large, flat area of land. Plains are mostly covered with grass and only a few trees. The ground has rich soil that is good for farming.

The area known as the Great Plains produces a lot of the food eaten in North America.

Land near water

The place where land meets water is called the coast or shore. A coast can drop down to the water over a cliff. It can also be flat and sandy with a beach. Coastlines surround islands. An island is an area of land with water all around it. Sometimes a coastline has a long, narrow strip of land that juts into the water. This is a peninsula.

A bay is water that has land almost all around it.

Where rivers meet the sea

When a river meets a lake or ocean, it can form a delta. A delta is often a triangle-shaped area. It is made of built up layers of soil. This soil is carried by the river and dropped at the **mouth** of the river. Some deltas are so big that people can live on them.

A delta is a place where a river splits into many channels. Those channels flow into a lake or an ocean.

Where is water found on Earth?

Water covers three-quarters of Earth's surface. Most of the water is in Earth's five oceans. An ocean is a large, deep body of salt water. The rest of the water on Earth is fresh water. Fresh water does not have salt in it. Lakes, streams, rivers, and ponds have fresh water.

There is also fresh water underground. People use pumps to bring the water up for drinking.

A stream is a small body of moving water. Many streams flow into rivers.

A river is long and narrow. It flows into a lake or ocean.

A lake is a large body of fresh water. A lake is surrounded by land on all sides.

A pond is a small body of still water. Ponds can form naturally or be made by people.

Frozen solid

Not all of Earth's water is liquid. Some of it is in solid form. Much of Earth's fresh water is frozen as ice in glaciers. Glaciers are thick layers of moving ice. Glaciers form when snow and **hail** begin to pile up high in the mountains. The weight causes the snow to change to ice. The ice then starts to slowly slide down the mountain.

The Perito Moreno glacier in Argentina is growing larger every year.

There are glaciers on every continent on Earth.

Frozen rivers

Glaciers push and drag rocks and soil down the mountain with them. Piles of soil and rock are left along the edges of the glacier. Glaciers carve out valleys as they move. The melted water from the glacier fills these landforms, creating rivers and lakes.

Models of Earth

Models are a way for us to study Earth. Maps are models that have landforms and bodies of water drawn on paper. Different colors show land and water. The same landforms are not found everywhere. One map might show an area with mountains and valleys. Another map might show an area with plains or large lakes.

Some maps can show a small area, such as a neighborhood, town, or city.

Other maps might show a large area, such as a country or even the whole world.

Globes help us see where in the world major landforms are found.

Take a good look

Globes are also models of Earth. However, globes are not flat like maps. They are **three-dimensional** models. Globes show the whole world.

What do you think?

To find the streams and ponds near your home, would you use a map or a globe? Why?

Making models

Earth is made up of many landforms. You can make your own model out of salt dough to see and better understand some of Earth's landforms.

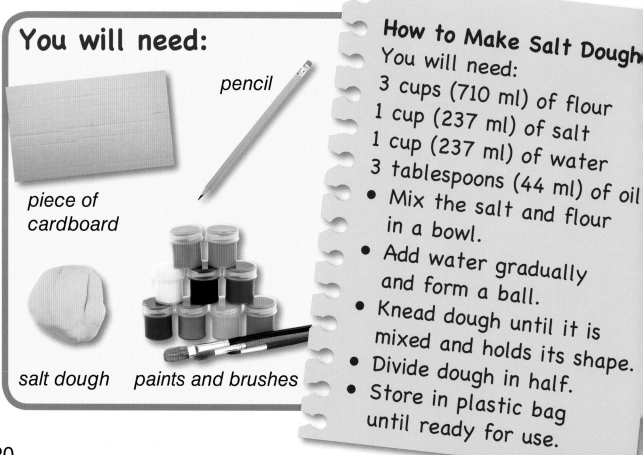

You will need:

pencil

piece of cardboard

salt dough

paints and brushes

How to Make Salt Dough
You will need:
3 cups (710 ml) of flour
1 cup (237 ml) of salt
1 cup (237 ml) of water
3 tablespoons (44 ml) of oil
- Mix the salt and flour in a bowl.
- Add water gradually and form a ball.
- Knead dough until it is mixed and holds its shape.
- Divide dough in half.
- Store in plastic bag until ready for use.

Steps

1. Search on the Internet for photos of "Physical Maps."

2. Choose a **region** or country to model. Try to find an area with at least four landforms.

3. Draw or trace the shape of your area on the cardboard.

4. Press some of the salt dough onto the cardboard. Flatten it to the outline of your region.

5. Using the map to guide you, add dough to build up raised landforms, such as hills, mountains, and plateaus.

6. Shape low landforms such as rivers and valleys.

7. Let your model dry for about 1 or 2 days.

8. Paint your landforms. Use different colors. Water can be blue. Then use different colors for higher sections. Green can be the lowest land, then yellow, then orange, and red for the highest land.

9. Add a color key to tell others what the colors mean.

21

Studying Earth

Geologists are scientists who study Earth's **features**. They look at rocks and soil to learn about Earth's history. They study landforms to see how they are changing Earth's surface. One way geologists do this is by making and studying models. Have a look at the model you made. How is your model the same as the real region? How is it different?

Rocks tells our Earth's history.

Learning more

Books

Introducing Landforms by Bobbie Kalman and Kelley MacAulay, Crabtree Publishing Company, 2008.

Comparing Bodies of Water by Rebecca Rissman, Heinemann, 2009.

What Is a Landform? by Rebecca Rissman, Heinemann, 2009.

Websites

Learn all about landforms at Geology For Kids:
www.kidsgeo.com/geology-for-kids/0031-what-are-landforms.php

Easy Science for Kids looks at bodies of water and how they are formed:
http://easyscienceforkids.com/tag/bodies-of-water/

This fun video teaches all about different landforms:
www.youtube.com/watch?v=KWTDmg8OI_Y

Words to know

concrete (KON-kreet) noun A mixture of gravel, sand, cement, and water that hardens into a strong material

features (FEE-chers) noun Interesting or important qualities

hail (heyl) noun Little beads of frozen rain

mouth [of a river] (mouth) noun The end of a river where it meets a lake or an ocean

region (REE-juh-n) noun An area or district

representation (rep-ri-zen-TEY-shuhn noun Something that stands in place of another thing with similar features

steep (steep) adjective At a high angle

three-dimensional (THREE-di-MEN-shuh-nl) adjective Something that has or seems to have, depth as well as length, width, and height

A *noun* is a person, place, or thing. An *adjective* is a word that tells you what something is like.

Index

bays 12
canyons 10
coastlines 12
deltas 13
fresh water 14, 15, 16
geologists 22
glaciers 16–17
gravel 6
hills 9, 10

lakes 4, 13, 14, 15, 17, 18
maps 5, 18, 19, 21
models 5, 18–19, 20–21, 22
mountains 4, 6, 7, 8, 9, 10, 16, 17, 18
oceans 4, 13, 14, 15
plains 4, 11, 18

plateaus 4, 9
ponds 4, 14, 15, 19
rivers 10, 13, 14, 15, 17
rocks 6, 17, 22
salt water 14
sand 6, 7, 12
soil 7, 10, 11, 13, 17, 22
streams 4, 14, 15, 19
valleys 4, 10, 17, 18